Hooked

poems by

Elizabeth K. Keggi

Finishing Line Press
Georgetown, Kentucky

Hooked

Copyright © 2022 by Elizabeth K. Keggi
ISBN 978-1-64662-826-1 First Edition
All rights reserved under International and Pan-American Copyright Conventions. No part of this book may be reproduced in any manner whatsoever without written permission from the publisher, except in the case of brief quotations embodied in critical articles and reviews.

ACKNOWLEDGMENTS

Grateful acknowledgements to
The Fox Cry Review for publishing "A Maid Is Never Idle," and to
The Wisconsin Fellowship of Poets for publishing "Spiders" on their website ("Honorable Mention" in The Triad Contest).

Publisher: Leah Huete de Maines
Editor: Christen Kincaid
Cover Art: Elizabeth K. Keggi
Author Photo: Peter C. Ducklow
Cover Design: Elizabeth Maines McCleavy

Order online: www.finishinglinepress.com
also available on amazon.com

Author inquiries and mail orders:
Finishing Line Press
PO Box 1626
Georgetown, Kentucky 40324
USA

Table of Contents

A Maid Is Never Idle 1

Convalescence 2

Sound Travels 3

No Diagnosis 4

Almost 5

Shadows' End 6

Hooked 7

Advent 9

Train 10

Ephemeral 11

The Hunt 12

The Leaves 13

Frozen 14

Return Notice 15

There's Always a Light at the End of the Tunnel 16

While Listening to Bach on His Reel-to-Reel 19

1970 20

Days Like This 21

Better the One You Know 22

Deconstruction 23

Between Sleep 24

Permanent Press 25

Spiders 26

Vanished 27

Death Follows Me 29

Orpheus in Oz 30

Screen Porch 31

Slow Motion 32

A Maid Is Never Idle
Based on the Vermeer painting
"Lady Writing a Letter with Her Maid"

My rough hands upon my arms—
but I am not thinking of laundry or potatoes

The weight of my dress—
but I am not thinking of mending

Every particle of dust lit by the sunlight—
but I am not thinking of furniture or rags

How I wished to pick up the letter
my mistress threw upon the floor!
But she forbade me to touch it
and so…

Boys outside kicking a ball and shouting—
and I am not thinking of scolding

The smell of candle wax and soot—
and I am not thinking of trimming wicks

I feel the movement of my breath—
I see the rough weave of the curtain
and the distortion of the glass—
I hear the scratch, scratch, scratch
of my mistress's pen—

I must let my lady fret—
passion is her own kind of pleasure

Convalescence

In the secret place within
beats a heart, a pump,
so frail at times
but consistent, a butterfly
here, there, pause, lift
feeding the flowers
pollen by pollen

A challenge lies ahead—
the floating of an afternoon nap
the safety of it

There's the danger
of waking too late—
hanging, hanging
the milkweed trembling
in the heat

The simplicity of it:
a white bandage
a cool cloth
a fever quenched

Better to be feverish
to rise, seeking water
to wander the empty rooms
wondering, Where did they go?

Hanging, hanging
by a thread
softly peeling open
edge by edge emerging.

Sound Travels

As I doze behind this gauzy curtained window,
shaded from the sun who gazes back,
the bed supports me and my dreaming,
and I know that I am loved.

Still, I rise and crack open
the window and the birds fly in—
a rush of blue and gold and Chinese lacquer red,
songs filling my room on wafts of thin air,

curling around my outstretched arms, my head;
whole hearts and whole music arise—
the ceiling vanishes and all above me is sky,
deep sky, singing its song of blue—No compromise,

just music on air skinnying up, and I don't know why.
I stand and watch the veils of song go 'round…
But I feel the floor solid beneath me—yes,
my travels will be steady and sound.

No Diagnosis

Here where there is no heat
just cold sunlight
drifting through the glass,
Here where the birds fly
from bush to branch
but never sing a note,
Here where cotton sheets
muffle the sound
of a body tossed & turned
by restless dreams—
Fear rises like a fire
on the horizon,
a bonfire's glow
searing the blackening sky
with its silent tongue.

Almost

I was almost too late
when you fell to the carpet,
crumpled to the floor,
eyes closed, mouth agape.
If I hadn't made that green light,
would I still have been there in time?
One red light, and it could have made
my love for you irrelevant.

Shadows' End

As sunlight streams from the tumbling sky
and casts its shapes around the shadows, I cast
my own outline upon the bed. Why,
I wonder, can't the body stretch to last?
My body wraps my soul with thinning, lined
skin. I contemplate its form and see
the tall trees hold the shadows behind
the small trees, a sight which pleases me.
Which sky will contain our end?
The black, the blue, or the simmering gray?
In dreams I see the sky sway and bend
and scoop me up like a child to play.
    If skies can cast their arms around us here,
    I know that there is nothing—ever—to fear.

Hooked

Most said he had it coming,
no-good trash, always into something,
always sent to the principal's office.
Sloppy speech, Goodwill clothes.
He liked to hop a ride on these trains.
He'd seen it done and decided to try it.
They go slow on the flats
so it's not too hard to catch up
and heave himself
into a dusty, greasy boxcar.

He loved the breeze up there,
the moving of time and space.
There were dusty, greasy men
in the boxcars at times.
They'd offer him tobacco and liquor
but didn't say much.
Their eyes were light with the miles
of tracks, the rocking,
the creak and clatter.

One day he slipped.
He was trying to show his friend,
his only friend, his new friend,
how to hop aboard,
But explaining broke the spell
of the waiting, the tensing,
the springing.
Thinking's what tripped him up.
The analyzing, the isolating.

He had a hook for an arm after that,
No more train hopping.
No more freedom.
Nothing to do but fight
like a caged animal.
The authorities sent him north
to prison for boys.

Somewhere there's a man
with a hook for an arm,
a man with a story. Or is there?
How does a boy survive?

Advent

If you give up too soon
the windows will darken
with frost—speckles, barbed lines—
snow closing in before you've even
donned your coat, your hat, and boots.
You forget to keep moving—
you crawl under covers
and listen, listlessly
for a sound that doesn't come.
The windows are etched—
the child not yet born—
sweet darkness
swept, but not yet.

Train

Train
train leaving town
the ribbon like a fish
skimming the stones

Red stones here
red granite
rough and beautiful
pretty enough to ponder

I shiver and tremble
the icy wind pushes hard—
no scarf, so I squint
and clench

What am I doing here?

The ribbon turns a corner

I hear the cacophonous call
"Leave," it says
"Leave." "Leave."

I wait

Ephemeral

I travel the path of newly budding trees,
palest green, like sherbet on a summer day—
but it is spring, I correct myself; see
how the birds bob up and down, swaying
with the songs of love and valor; branches
nearly naked, flexible and light as feathers.
The perennials are finally taking their chances
as they burst from the warming soil, whether
or not the clouds bring snow instead of rain.
It's pointless now, any hesitation of purples and reds;
The bumblebees are hard at work, and the plain
jane gnats make love in frantic circles until they're dead.
    Such brief lives—procreate and then they're done:
    Next year's spring has already begun.

The Hunt

Light creeps through the valley
a meandering dusk, treading a careful
path between the trees and settling
on the hostas and ferns with a peculiar glow.

The sky is fading orange and purple until
only a peach-pink streak remains,
and the birds grow quiet, waiting
for the owl to declare its territory.

The owl now flaps her wings and settles
atop the tallest tree in the ravine.
The sky is gray now, with only the brightest stars
poking through. The trees are a block of shadows.

Night hangs thick, like a tapestry.
Crickets sing below, the stars humming above,
and rabbits, silent as the foxes,
nibble on the wet grass.

The Leaves

August fullness of green
and cicada songs in the tree
give way, leaf by leaf
to a colder sun.
The tips of the maples
chatter with their dry
congregation looking down
down on me.
There are no reds or blazing
orange leaves celebrating
then falling at my feet
like scraps of poster paint.
It's all gone gray.
Gray chatter, gray condemnation
gray evidence at every step.
As I shuffle through
the autumn fallout
the trees are raining ashes
and my stride slows until
I'm mumbling to myself,
eyes fixed on the ground
ground as gray as winter skies
the evidence sticking to my shoes.

Frozen

As we trudge our way to the icy lake,
you tell me at last about your news:
two years of loving another; for my sake
you kept quiet. I knew, but I choose
to keep my secrets on this winter trail.
I look around: No life to be seen
here as the light begins to fail.
The wind is cold, the ground cover lean.
But I spy tracks of a rabbit in the snow!
And there she is, in a coat of white,
trembling by a fallen branch, no
safety in the late-day light.
    A hawk's aloft now, in search of prey;
    The rabbit tenses, unable to run away.

Return Notice

Like the books I check out
from the library
usually on hold for weeks
while I wait for each reader
to release the book
from her avid grasp,
you are but on loan to me,
nonrenewable,
because when my time's up
another woman waits
to slip you into her bag
and take you home.

There's always a light at the end of the tunnel

My grandparents lived in Manhattan
in a stuffy old apartment with rusty water
and knocking pipes. My uncle lived there too,
always ready for a drink and a fight.
I learned to sip my ginger ale in the library
that doubled as my uncle's room.
A funny place, a bedroom with two doors.
My brothers and I read books and played Life.

My brothers knew where all the graveyards were
from New Jersey to Manhattan.
We were ready, all three, to heave air into our lungs
when my oldest brother shouted "Now!"
He could always hold his breath the longest,
but by the time I was six, I had learned
how to hold my own against these ghosts
who tried to snatch our souls.
I didn't know any dead people then,
but I was young enough to believe my brothers.

The Holland Tunnel lay ahead.
Who would be the first whose lungs gave out?
Thirteen men died building the tunnel beneath
the Hudson River—my brothers told me so.
I always wondered
would the walls cave in this time too?
Water and mud pressed on those rounded walls,
shiny white tiles, uncountable, that I hoped weren't cracked
like the ones in my grandparents' bathroom.
I was the smallest so I always drowned first--
the tunnel was too long.

We never held our breath on the way home.
My brothers lost interest by then, but I secretly
held my breath when they wouldn't notice and tease.
I still feared the river and the ghosts. I knew
The Hudson River would be my grave.

I slept on the sofa, trying not to roll off
the slippery leather cushions, the window
above my head always open, just a crack.
City lights penetrated the blinds and
the sound of a jackhammer—always a jackhammer—
peppered in the distance. I had never realized
that men worked at night, that the
construction never ends.

Twenty years later, I watched the men
throw a shovel of dirt each onto
my grandmother's coffin,
I wondered at the dullness of the sound—
My victory had been hollow after all.
Anger wrapped around me like
the waters of the Hudson,
and I was young enough to believe
I was rid of them at last,
rid of them all.

The Hudson River is pressing upon
the veins that slip beneath the river.
I tried so hard to make it through.
I've got their blood in my veins,
my grandparents' blood.
We all held our breath—even my mother
whenever we entered Manhattan
and returned, suffocated, every time.

*I'm old enough to know,
to know now at last that ghosts can be
shed like a rattlesnake's skin.
You rub and you slither
until they let go, and
let the sun burn them dry.*

While listening to Bach on his reel-to-reel

My father patiently writes in black ink,
sits on his couch on the end by his desk,

ring binders, papers laid out just so.
Bach turns serenely on the reel-to-reel

while the tiny black-and-white TV,
perched quietly among the books, waits

for The MacNeil/Lehrer Report.
Bourbon on the rocks, the clink of ice,

his handwriting straight as a typewriter's,
an even and elegant calligraphic scrawl,

while I peer in, waiting for my chance
to watch Jim Lehrer in solemn silence

and comprehend nothing, save one thing:
I am in, I am near, I'm almost here.

1970

As the movers shuffled in and out
we were struck by their lack of intelligence
in the matter of packing the truck just so.
My mother and I stepped aside outside the door
to let them pass with a dresser in their grip.
I nearly stumbled into the garden.
"Ma'am," said one of them when they paused,
"I don't know if you know this,
but that's marijuana you're growing there."
Later that day, they dropped the piano.

Days Like This

There have been days like this
When grass whispers to grass
Bowing and bending like
Old men with secrets,
the sky such an effortless blue.

Is it a miracle that we forget
days like these?
The air washed clean
by last night's storm,
the sun on our faces
the breeze making
the ladies' hats quiver.

Oh, such a nice day for a wedding!—
we say at the end. But later
we only examine the pictures
to see whom we resemble.

Better the one you know

As I carefully wrap the remains of your conversation,
a monologue with morsels of interjections by me,
I draw close to the half-curtained window:
the moon's split in two, with raggedy edges,
pockmarked like a demon who scratches at his wounds.
As your fragrance lingers at the stove,
or in the bedroom where I keep the bedclothes
clean and bright, you hover in the air like stale
cigarette smoke winding its way to my lungs,
then drifting deeper, to the source of breath—
and I catch myself grasping for a song, an aria of fire
to burn your mark from my heart.
The moon leers at me, that old devil,
and I scan the sky for friendlier faces,
but even Venus has vanished beneath her inscrutable veils.
Dinner's done, and you've left me again—
yet I can't bear to shake the crumbs into the night air.

Deconstruction

A lie's bitter
aftertaste cuts deep
into the throat—
Lies upon lies
burrow to the belly
and twist
sharply

until
internal
harmony
collapses on itself—
Nerves, organs fall,
a cascade of bones,
a pool of dust to kick;

Lies beget lies,
parading as love
and affection, and
kisses on lips—
just like when I
reach
for you.

Between sleep

Sleep spreads its sticky fingers
from behind the ribs,
swallows all the bones
to reveal the rounding breasts
prickling beneath the sheets.

Sleep spreads slowly,
tracing the blood, its blue-veined paths
arched like lightning
between two skies.

As if sleep were a matter
of curves and simple questions,
questions, and not just rest
recovering in the damp hollows
between the sheets—
as if the jaw weren't clenched.

Permanent Press

Scandal—a sensation—
splashed across the printed
sheets, the flannel sheets
you crushed with your feet
as you climbed upon my bed.
But by afternoon
I was humming with the
tumble dryer, set on Hot
for speedy, creaseless return.

Spiders

Spiders hide themselves
in silent spots deep
within the closet,
beneath the bed,
between the window
and the screen.

Spiders know
when you are asleep:
They are drawn
from their nests
by the sweet sound of a
little boy's gentle breath.

They're in the light
fixture above your head.
They guard the bathroom,
waiting for that midnight
visit made on your soft
bare feet in the dark.

Good little boys have
rooms free of spiders
and midnight venom.
Were you a good
little boy today?
I think not.

Vanished

The creeping light
came and swallowed me whole
tucked me into his folds of morning air
and we retreated from the room.

Where are you taking me?
We're on a wild ride.
The light is deceptively soft
as the pale blue sky is at rest.
But I'll be riding the sun
on his rollicking journey
across the sky.
I laugh when I see
the life-giving sun playing his tricks:
Sandy beaches too hot to walk on;
White skin turning brown then red;
cataracts; dead babies in hot cars--
The more the merrier, he laughs,
that cowboy in the sky.

And when he slips beneath the horizon
he releases me ever so gently
and I slowly roll back into bed
under covers, under darkness
asleep as if the damage was never done.

Night peels the heat
away from my skin.
She tousles my hair
and arranges my limbs
in the most restful position.
She could be up to mischief
but tonight she is like a mother
tending to her little scamp.

She fills the room with her infinite body
and I breathe her in and out
her soft weight holding me down
as the world inside me rights itself:

Breathe in, breathe out
Knowing that I am loved
especially when I sleep in her arms.

Death follows me

Death follows me
wherever I go
strewing red roses
in my wake.
That inscrutable shadow
in a black, black cloak
stepping lightly as a girl.
I swear I can see
her rosy cheeks
dusted by sunlight
when I look over
my shoulder.

Orpheus in Oz

I walk with love,
and music lays
the yellow brick road
to the walled city
where you have been taken.

I burst with song, and
the Flying Monkeys
grow still, hang back
in the trees, jabbering softly
as I sing your name.

The woman at the gate
is a regular Helen Keller
no music could ever reach her deaf ears
and she repels my touch
as I urgently sign your name
into her hand in a language
I didn't know I knew.

Tap your heels three times,
she signs at last, and she
demonstrates it herself.
There's no place like home,
she insists over and over
in my eager palm.

And home's where I find you.
You came back.
Did you hear me sing your name?
All this time, and you came back.
And unlike poor Dorothy,
we're in full Technicolor.
I can see your ruby slippers
and I have to laugh.
Kansas never looked so good.

Screen Porch

Paris was never like this.
Warm nights in a dark, leafy garden
fat rabbits move about the yard
unseen and unheard
while far off I can hear the hum
of trucks on 441.
Something scrabbles against the fence
and the TV is just audible
from out here on the porch--
You are learning about barbecuing
while I assemble my summer reading list
from the New York Times Book Review.
A breeze lolls through the trees
like a canoe in still waters,
the leaves giving way as it passes through.
In the morning the birds will be singing
from every direction, and the sun
will stretch across my legs as I write this poem.

Slow Motion

> "It's the end of the world as we know it,
> and I feel fine." —R.E.M.

I.
As your car sails toward the wayward semi,
no chance of stopping in time,
I consider whether death might be like this:
A soft sinking into one's seat; a relaxation
of muscles clenched for years.
Thinking about the person next to you
and how good it was to have known them
if only for a little while.

II.
We inch closer, just a couple of car lengths now,
and you're pulling hard to the right.
All things considered, life's been good.
Childhood abuses fall behind; confusion, headaches,
hallucinations, all released with a deep sigh.
All is forgiven. No more regrets.
One long last look at you, and then I close my eyes.

III.
I long to kiss you again, once the shards
of glass and metal have been extracted
and the last clumps of sod thrown down.
We'll walk hand-in-hand beyond
the roadside crosses, into the grassy field
beyond the ditch, and no one can stop us.
You will crown me with wildflowers—
No burdens to separate us because I'll
have been liberated at last. Shall we walk on?

Elizabeth Keggi is a lifelong musician, reader, and writer. She works with dyslexic children and teens in the Appleton, Wisconsin area and loves opening the doors to reading and writing for her students.

www.ingramcontent.com/pod-product-compliance
Lightning Source LLC
LaVergne TN
LVHW041507070426
835507LV00012B/1381